KT-159-487

WHIZZY SCIENCE

Make it Bang!

Written by:
Anna Claybourne

Illustrated by:
Kimberley Scott and Venetia Dean

First published in 2013 by Wayland
Copyright © Wayland 2013

Wayland
338 Euston Road
London NW1 3BH

Wayland Australia
Hachette Children's Books
Level 17/207
Kent Street
Sydney, NSW 2000

All rights reserved.

Senior Editor: Julia Adams
Designer: Anthony Hannant (LittleRedAnt)
Illustrator (step-by-steps): Kimberley Scott
Illustrator (incidentals and final crafts): Venetia Dean
Proofreader & Indexer: Sara Harper

The website addresses (URLs) included in this book were valid at the time of going to press. However, it is possible that contents or addresses may have changed since the publication of this book. No responsibility for any such changes can be accepted by either the author or the Publisher.

Dewey categorisation: 534

ISBN 978 0 7502 7731 0

Printed in China

Wayland is a division of Hachette Children's Books,
an Hachette UK company.

www.hachette.co.uk

Picture acknowledgements:
All photographs: Shutterstock; except: p. 17: iStockphoto.

N E LINCS LIBRARIES

5 4073 010337212

NORT

AUTH

Contents

BANG!!!

What makes things go BANG? Or crash, clatter, squeak, creak, hoot or any other sound? The answer is movement. Sound is a kind of energy that comes from things moving and shaking quickly to and fro – also known as vibrating.

TA-TA-TAAAAA

WHIZZZZ

RAT-A-TAT RAT-A-TAT

RUMBLE RUMBLE

WHIZZZZ

ZIP

LIKE WHAT?

Things vibrate in different ways to make all kinds of sounds.

BANG! If you bang a door shut, it vibrates suddenly, making a loud, short noise.

CRASH! Hitting a cymbal makes the metal vibrate with a loud crashing sound.

Laaaaaa! When you sing or talk, you blow air through stringy bits of muscle in your throat, and they vibrate.

INTO YOUR EARS

Sound wave

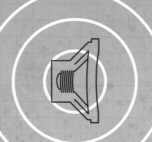

Of course, we only know what all these sounds are like because we can hear them. They spread out through the air and go into our ears, which are specially built to detect them. Hearing is amazingly useful – it helps us talk to each other, send long-distance messages, spot danger, and enjoy TV, films and music.

BEING A SCIENTIST

This book is packed full of fun experiments to try with bangs, crashes and other sounds, to help you find out how sounds work. To get the best results, here are a few sound science tips:

1. Set up your experiments according to the instructions and watch carefully to see what happens.

2. To be like a real scientist, write down your results in a notebook.

3. Scientists often do experiments several times over, to check they always work the same way.

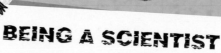

5

see a bang

Everything that makes a sound is moving, but you can't always see the vibrations that make sound. This experiment makes it a bit easier to spot them!

YOU WILL NEED

1) An empty food container
2) Clingfilm or a plastic bag
3) Long elastic bands
4) A pencil or wooden spoon
5) Rice grains

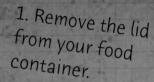
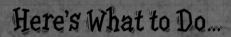

Here's What to Do...

1. Remove the lid from your food container.

2. Stretch a large piece of the plastic bag tightly around the container, and hold it in place with elastic bands.

3. Sprinkle a pinch of rice onto the surface of your 'drum'.

4. Bang the drum gently with a pencil or wooden spoon.

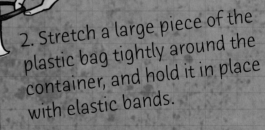

WHAT'S GOING ON?

When you hit the drum, it makes the plastic skin vibrate very quickly up and down. It's hard to see, because the vibrations are quite small and fast. But if there are rice grains sitting on top, the vibrations make them jump up and down, showing you what's happening.

TROUBLESHOOTER

The plastic should be very tight and smooth. You may need two people to put it on – one to hold it while the other fixes it in place.

WHAT NEXT?

Do the rice grains behave differently if you put them near the edge or right in the middle?

Try making a loud noise just above the drum without touching it (shout, clap or bang things together) – can you make the rice grains jump? Why does this happen?

Bang, twang, pop

Try making some loud and peculiar noises using some of the everyday objects around you. See if you can work out why they sound different from each other.

YOU WILL NEED
1) Wooden blocks, bricks or chopping boards
2) A ruler
3) A balloon
4) A coin with lots of sides (a screw nut with six sides also works)

1. Clap your hands, stamp your feet, or bang two blocks of wood together.

2. Put your finger in your mouth, close it tightly, blow hard, then pop your finger out sideways.

3. Hold a ruler firmly over the edge of a table, and twang the free end.

4. Put a multi-sided coin inside a balloon, blow it up and tie it, then twirl it around to make the coin roll fast around the inside.

8

WHAT'S GOING ON?

All these activities involve hitting or somehow moving an object to make it vibrate. The sound the object makes depends on how it moves, and what it is made of. Springy or rubbery objects such as the ruler and the balloon skin tend to make more twangy, long-lasting sounds, as they bounce to and fro. Hard, rigid objects such as wooden blocks stop vibrating more quickly, and make short, sharp sounds.

Can you make a hooting owl sound with your hands? Cup them together, with a gap between your thumbs, and blow gently across the gap.

DID YOU KNOW?

If there is air inside a vibrating object, the air will vibrate too, adding to the sound.

WHAT NEXT?

Write down descriptions of each sound – are they high or low, loud or quiet, spooky, funny or strange?

How a bang travels

Why can we hear sound? Because it travels from the moving object to our ears, in the form of sound waves. This experiment shows how sound waves work.

YOU WILL NEED

1) A metal or plastic slinky or spiral spring toy
2) A smooth, hard floor
3) At least two people

Here's What to Do...

1. Stretch the spring out along the floor, with a person at each end holding it still.

2. One person should give their end a sharp push, then move it back to its starting position.

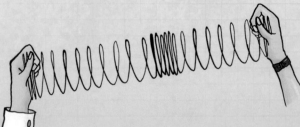

3. You should see the movement zoom all the way along the spring to the other person's hand!

WHAT'S GOING ON?

When you push the end of the spring, the first coil pushes the next coil, which pushes the next one, and so on. In this way the energy of the push moves right along the spring.

TROUBLESHOOTER

The spring needs to be spread out, but not pulled too tight; experiment to find the best amount of stretch.

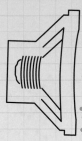

Sound waves in air work the same way. When something vibrates, it pushes against the tiny molecules in the air around it, making them vibrate too. They push the molecules next to them, and they push the molecules next to them, and so on.

BOUNCING BACK

An echo is a sound wave that has bounced off a surface. If you can tape one end of your spring to a wall, you may be able to recreate this, too.

WHAT NEXT?

Can you send a series of waves all at once, one following another?

Can you recreate how a sound wave travels using a line of people?

The speed of a bang

You hit a drum or shut a door, and you hear a sound – BANG! It seems as if it happens straight away. But actually it takes time for sound to travel to your ears. So how fast does it go?

YOU WILL NEED

1) A tape measure or measuring wheel
2) Two bin lids, pan lids or cymbals
3) A stopwatch
4) A pen and paper
5) A calculator
6) At least two people

Here's What to Do...

1. Measure out a 250 m distance on a flat playing field, park or beach.

250 m

2. One person should stand 250 m away from the other, and bang the lids or cymbals together.

3. The other person should start the timer when they see the bang happening, and stop it when they hear the bang. You'll need to react quickly!

4. Write down how long the bang takes to travel 250 m. From this you can calculate the speed of sound (see What's Going On?).

WHAT'S GOING ON?

When the lids bang, the sound starts to spread out through the air. You see it happen almost immediately, as the speed of light is very, very fast. But sound is much slower. If you are 250 m away, it should take about 0.7 seconds to reach you.

To find the speed of sound in metres per second, divide 250 by your result.

For example, 250 divided by 0.73 = about 342 metres per second.

This is the same as about 1,235 kilometres per hour (or 768 miles per hour) – as fast as a very fast jet plane. Zoom!

! TROUBLESHOOTER

You need a calm day – avoid noisy wind and rain!

THUNDER AND LIGHTNING

In a thunderstorm, lightning makes the sound of thunder. But if the storm is far away, you see the lightning first, then hear the CRACK! when the sound reaches you.

WHAT NEXT?

Do the experiment several times to get a good average measurement.

Can you do it over an even bigger distance?

Bangs and whispers

Why are some sounds loud and others quiet? Try making sounds of different volumes and see if you can work out what's happening.

YOU WILL NEED

1) A drum and drumstick, or a pan and a wooden spoon
2) Musical instruments, if you have any
3) Everyday objects
4) A pen and paper

Here's What to Do...

1. Try making loud and quiet bangs on your drum or pan.

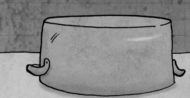

2. Try making loud and quiet sounds on a musical instrument or by singing.

3. Try clapping, rubbing objects together, or rattling a box with something inside.

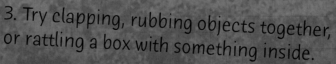

4. Write down what you have to do to make sound louder in each experiment.

WHAT'S GOING ON?

Whatever you're using to make a sound, making it louder always involves the same thing. Did you notice what it was? Sound is a form of energy, and louder sounds carry more energy, as they involve stronger vibrations. So to make louder sounds, you have to put more energy in. That means hitting, blowing or shaking harder. Put in a lot less energy, and you get a really quiet sound instead.

SOUND SCALE

Scientists measure how loud sounds are using the decibel or dB scale. Very quiet sounds, like rustling leaves, measure about 20 dB. Super-loud sounds like a jet taking off are around 140 dB.

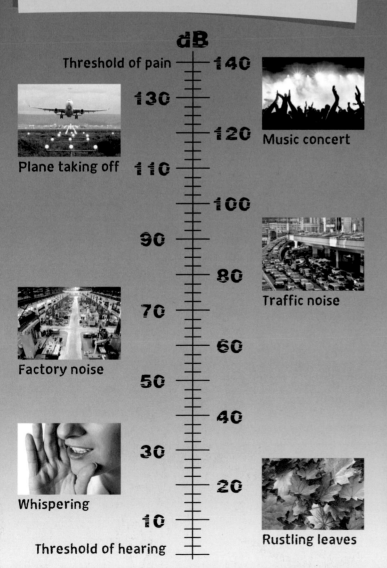

dB

Threshold of pain — 140

130

120 — Music concert

Plane taking off — 110

100

90

80 — Traffic noise

70

Factory noise — 60

50

40

30

Whispering — 20 — Rustling leaves

10

Threshold of hearing

WHAT NEXT?

Experiment with the plastic drum skin and rice grains from page 6. Do the rice grains behave differently when you bang the drum skin harder?

Whispering is another way to be quiet, but to do this, you stop your voice from making a sound, and just use your breath. How quietly can you talk without whispering?

The SCreaming CUP

How can you make a cup shriek and squawk like a parrot? It might seem pretty unlikely, but here's how to do it...

Here's What to Do...

YOU WILL NEED

1) A clean, dry paper cup
2) A sharp pencil
3) A candle
4) Thread

1. Make a small hole in the base of the cup, using a sharp pencil (ask an adult to help).

2. Cut a 30-cm long piece of thread and thread it through the hole, then knot the end so it's held in place.

"SQUAWK!"

3. Rub the candle up and down the thread to make it waxy.

4. Hold the cup in one hand, and pull on the thread with the other, so that your hand slips down it.

WHAT'S GOING ON?

As your fingers slip down the thread in sudden jerks and jumps, they make it vibrate. The vibrations are small and you would normally hardly hear anything. But as the thread is connected to the cup, it makes the cup vibrate too, along with the air inside it. This makes a louder sound... ...which sounds a bit like a squawking parrot!

squawk!

PAPER CUP PHONE CALL

A paper cup telephone works in the same way. You use a long piece of string to join two cups together, then stretch it tight. When you speak into one cup, the vibrations travel along the string and into the other cup, making it sound as if the other person is right next to you!

AMPLIFICATION

Making sounds louder is called amplifying them.

! TROUBLESHOOTER

If it doesn't work, try gripping the thread with a damp paper towel.

WHAT NEXT?

What happens if you put the cup to your ear and tap the bottom of it?

Try cutting the bottom off a paper cup and speaking through it.

17

High and low

How high or low a sound is, is called its pitch. Every sound has a pitch, and musical instruments and voices can change their pitch. How do they do it?

YOU WILL NEED
1) A clean, empty glass bottle
2) Water
3) A spoon
4) A wide, shallow box or tray, like a baking tray
5) A long elastic band

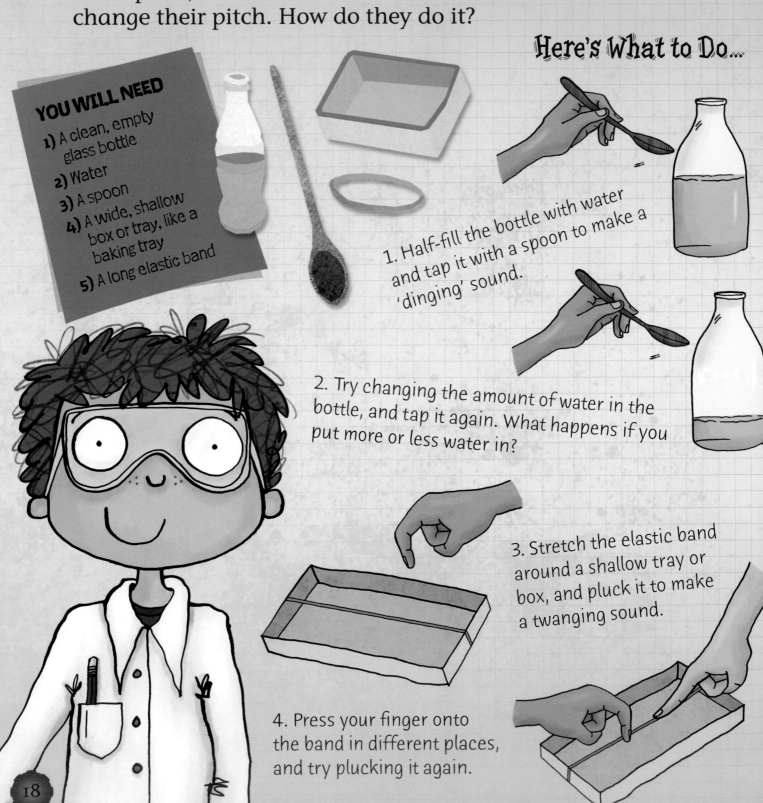

1. Half-fill the bottle with water and tap it with a spoon to make a 'dinging' sound.

2. Try changing the amount of water in the bottle, and tap it again. What happens if you put more or less water in?

3. Stretch the elastic band around a shallow tray or box, and pluck it to make a twanging sound.

4. Press your finger onto the band in different places, and try plucking it again.

WHAT'S GOING ON?

With both these experiments, you are changing the pitch of a sound. You are actually doing this by making the vibrations faster or slower. When there's less air in the bottle, it makes shorter and faster vibrations, and a higher-pitched sound. When the elastic band is shorter, it vibrates to and fro faster, and its pitch is higher.

HOW MANY HERTZ?

Pitch is measured by the number of vibrations per second, also called Hertz, or Hz. For example, the top string on a guitar is about 330 Hz, meaning it vibrates 330 times every second – quite fast!

WHAT NEXT?

You can blow across the top of the bottles to make a different sound – but is it the same pitch?

If you have several bottles the same size and shape, you can use different amounts of water to 'tune' them to different notes, and make a bottle xylophone. What tunes can you play?

The sounds of speech

You always have one musical instrument with you – your voice! Find out how you make it go up and down, and why.

YOU WILL NEED

1) Not much! Just your voice and your hands.

Here's What to Do...

1. Put your fingers gently on your throat, like this.

2. Sing loudly, starting very low, and moving up to a high note, then back down.

3. Now change between singing a note, and blowing while making no sound.

20

WHAT'S GOING ON?

Your voice is made by two bands of muscle in your throat called vocal cords or vocal folds. To make your voice higher, they stretch, so that they are tighter and vibrate faster. When you sing low, they are looser and vibrate more slowly. Parts of your throat have to move around to change their position, and you can feel this with your hand.

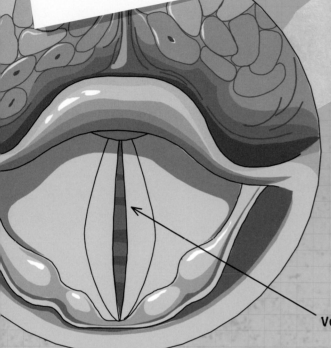

Vocal cords together make a sound.

! TROUBLESHOOTER

You might need to move your hand around a bit at first to find the best position.

You can also move your vocal cords apart so that they don't vibrate at all. This happens when you blow, whisper or breathe normally. When they're together, you can feel the vibrations, but when they are apart, the vibrations stop.

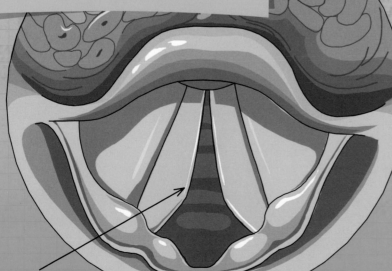

Vocal cords apart for breathing.

WHAT NEXT?

Think about what pitch is for – why is it useful for our voices to go up and down?

Try speaking without changing pitch at all. It's hard!

Try saying one word, such as 'yes', 'no' or 'OK', but using pitch to give it different meanings – for example try to sound keen, bored or rude. See if other people understand you!

Solid sounds

Sounds travel differently through solid objects, such as spoons, string and fingers than they do through the air. Find out what happens with this dangling, jangling spoon experiment!

YOU WILL NEED

1) String
2) A metal spoon
3) A table or other hard object

Here's What to Do...

1. Tie a 30-cm long piece of string to the handle of a metal spoon.

2. Wrap the other end of the string around your finger a few times, and bang the spoon gently against a table to make a ringing noise.

3. Now do the same thing again, but with the finger with the string around it pressed against your ear. Does it sound any different?

WHAT'S GOING ON?

When the sound just travels from the spoon through the air to your ears, it's quieter. When it travels along the spoon, the string and your finger into your ear, it sounds louder and a bit more detailed. Solid things actually carry sounds better and faster than air does.

There's a simple reason for this – solids contain more molecules than air, and they're more tightly packed together. This means sound vibrations pass from one molecule to the next more easily and quickly.

SAFETY WARNING

Press your finger gently against your ear, but DON'T stick it right inside – it's not very good for you.

Solid

Liquid

Gas

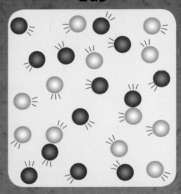

You could try this experiment with other solid objects, too, such as a ruler or a plastic cup. What works best?

FEELING FOR SOUNDS

Deaf people can sometimes get a better sense of sounds by touching the vibrating object to pick up the sound vibrations. Percussion player Evelyn Glennie, for example, performs with bare feet to help her sense vibrations through the ground.

WHAT NEXT?

What happens if you put your ears under the water in the bath while the tap is running? Sound also travels better through liquids than in air, as liquids have more molecules.

stop that Langing

Sometimes, you want to stop sound and keep it quiet. In fact, sometimes loud noises can be a problem. So what's the best way to block out sounds?

Here's What to Do...

YOU WILL NEED

1) Three tallish cardboard boxes
2) Cotton wool
3) Craft glue
4) Modelling clay
5) A small bell or whistle

1. Take one box and stick a thick layer of cotton wool all over the inside of it, using the glue.

2. Press a layer of modelling clay all over the inside of the second box.

3. Leave one box empty.

4. Ring a small bell or blow a whistle inside each box. Do they sound different?

24

WHAT'S GOING ON?

Sound bounces and echoes off some surfaces, but gets absorbed or soaked up by others. The softer and woollier the surface, the better it is at soaking up sound and making it seem quieter. We use this muffling effect for soundproofing – trying to stop unwanted sounds from spreading.

TROUBLESHOOTER

For it to work well the boxes should all be the same size.

BLOCK YOUR EARS!

Really loud sounds can damage your hearing, so people who work with loud noises need to protect their ears. Ear defenders like these block out sound with several layers of foam, wool or rubber.

Earplugs, made of squishy foam-like material, fit just inside the ears. Ear defenders sit over the top of your ears to block out sound.

WHAT NEXT?

What makes the best sound insulation? Try other materials too, such as cardboard, felt, tissue paper or a woolly sock.

When would sound insulation be useful? Think about where you would put it to keep a bedroom quiet at night, or stop the sounds of music escaping from a recording studio.

find the bang

Can you tell which direction a sound is coming from?
If you have two ears you can, and often do! How is
that possible?

YOU WILL NEED
1) A scarf or eye mask to use as a blindfold
2) A chair
3) A group of at least four people

Here's What to Do...

1. One person should put on the blindfold and sit in the chair.

2. The others should stand in a ring around the chair, and take turns to make a noise.

3. The listener should try to point to where each noise is coming from.

WHAT'S GOING ON?

We use the fact that we have two ears to detect the direction of sounds. As sound takes time to travel, it reaches your ears at very slightly different times. You don't notice this, but your brain can tell! It uses the information to help it work out where sounds are coming from.

The outer part of your ear helps too. Its shape reflects sounds into your ear in different patterns depending on what direction they come from. Again, your brain can spot these tiny differences.

SATELLITE EARS

The sticking-out part of your ear, called the pinna, works a bit like a satellite dish to catch sounds and bounce them into your ears. It also protects your earhole from wind, rain and dirt!

TROUBLESHOOTER

Don't stand too close to the chair – stand back, a few steps away

WHAT NEXT?

What happens if the person in the chair covers up one of their ears? Does the task become harder?

Take turns so that everyone has a go on the chair. Are some people better than others at spotting where sounds come from?

How musical are you?

Some people find it easy to listen to and remember tunes, while others find it almost impossible. Test yourself and your friends!

YOU WILL NEED
1) A piano, xylophone or electronic keyboard.
2) A scarf or eye mask to use as a blindfold

Here's What to Do...

1. The person being tested should put on the blindfold and face away from the keyboard.

2. Play two different notes on the keyboard, fairly close together, one after the other.

3. Ask the listener if they know whether the notes have moved up or down in pitch.

4. If they get that right, ask them how many keys apart the notes were.

28

WHAT'S GOING ON?

The ability to hear tunes and different notes is partly in your genes, meaning you are born with it. It can also be affected by how much you have learned about music. However, a few people – around 4 out of every 100 – simply cannot do it, however hard they try! Their brains simply don't work that way.

TROUBLESHOOTER

Make sure the blindfold doesn't cover the person's ears!

PERFECT PITCH

Some people have an ability called perfect pitch, which means they can actually name a particular note when they hear it.

WHAT'S THAT RACKET?

There are a few people who cannot understand musical sounds at all. To them, music just sounds like a jumble of noises, and some even find it upsetting. This condition is called amusia.

WHAT NEXT?

Test to see if anyone can sing the exact notes they have heard. If they can manage two notes easily, see if they can sing three, four or five in a row.

Glossary

amplify To make a sound louder.

amusia Inability to make sense of music.

decibel (dB) Unit used to measure how loud a sound is.

ear defenders Ear covers for blocking out loud sounds.

earplugs Small plugs that fit inside the ears to block out sounds.

echo Sound that has hit a surface and bounced off it.

energy The power to do work or make things happen.

Hertz (Hz) Unit used to measure pitch, or how high or low a sound is.

molecules The tiny units that materials are made of.

perfect pitch Ability to recognize and name musical notes by their sound.

pinna The sticking-out part of the ear that you can see.

pitch How high or low a sound is.

sound waves Patterns of sound vibrations that spread out through a substance.

soundproofing Muffling sound to stop it from spreading.

vibrate To shake very quickly to and fro.

vocal cords or vocal folds Bands of muscle in the throat that vibrate to make voice sounds.

further reading

BOOKS

Make and Use: Musical Instruments
by Anna-Marie D'Cruz, Wayland, 2010

Experiments with Sound and Hearing
by Chris Woodford, Gareth Stevens
Publishing, 2010

Science Detective Investigates: Sound
by Harriet McGregor, Wayland, 2011

Bang! Sound And How We Hear Things
by Peter Riley, Franklin Watts, 2012

WEBSITES

Zoom Science: Sound
http://pbskids.org/zoom/activities/
sci/#sound

**Neuroscience for Kids: Hearing
Experiments**
http://faculty.washington.edu/chudler/
chhearing.html

Index

Whizzy SCIENCE

Titles in the series:

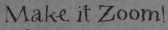

Make it Zoom!
978 0 7502 7732 7

Zooming cars
Straw shooter
Heli-zoomer
Zero-gravity water squirt
Zooming balloon rocket
Magazine tug-of-war
Jelly slide
Flying bucket
Whirling wind speed meter
Ping pong flinger
Gas-fuelled rocket
Magnet power

Make it Bang!
978 0 7502 7731 0

See a bang
Bang, twang, pop!
How a bang travels
The speed of a bang
Bangs and whispers
The screaming cup
High and low
The sounds of speech
Solid sounds
Stop that banging!
Find the bang
How musical are you?

Make it Change!
978 0 7502 7734 1

Turn a penny green!
Lava volcano
The red cabbage test
Exploding drinks
Make salt disappear –
   and reappear
Rubbery bones
Bottle balloon
Magic ice cubes
Plastic bag ice cream
Pure water still
Make your own butter
Mould garden

Make it Grow!
978 0 7502 7736 5

Egg-head!
What makes plants grow?
Supermarket sprout!
Black bag balloon
Make a thermometer
Expanding ice
Sugary strings
Grow your own stalactites
Microwave a marshmallow
Popcorn!
Make bread rise
Squirty cream challenge

Make it Glow!
978 0 7502 7733 4

Light and shadows
Periscope
Tea light lanterns
Make an indoor rainbow
Glowing envelopes, plasters
   and sweets!
Glow-in-the-dark shapes
Make a glowing jar lantern
Glow stick photos
Glowing water stream
Laser jelly
Camera obscura
Ultraviolet glow

Make it Splash!
978 0 7502 7735 8

Make a splash
Does water have a skin?
Upside-down cup
Water balloon pop!
Why do boats float?
Rising raisins
Magic liquid levels
Melted crayon art
The saliva test
Make your own river
Strange gloop
More water fun